Table Of Contents

MW00958779

Setting up your iPhone

Switching on your device

Press and hold the iPhone's power button until the Apple logo appears. The word Hello will appear on the screen in many languages. Follow the simple steps below to start using your device.

When the option to select your preferred language appears, tap your country or region. Your selection will automatically affect the appearance of certain information on your device such as date, time, contacts, etc. Tap the accessibility tab in blue to set up various Accessibility Options.

1. Tap the accessibility knob on your Quick Start Screen
2. Tap the accessibility option to view details about the feature and switch it on. Press the Back button to return to the previous options
3. Press the Done to return to the setup process

If you do not have another device with iOS 12.4 or later, press Set Up Manually to proceed.

How to directly transfer data from your iPhone to another device

If your previous iPhone and the new device both use iOS 12.4 or later; the iPhone migration feature allows you to transfer data directly between devices without the need for cables if your wireless connection is high-speed. However, a wired option is also available if your network is slow or congested.

For wireless data transfer, both devices must be placed side by side or in close proximity until the process is completed. Ensure that your iPhones are connected to a power source.

For wired data transfer, use a Lightning to USB Camera Adapter and a Lightning to USB cable. Insert the Lightning to USB 3

Camera Adapter to your old device, then connect the Lightning to USB Cable to your new device. Plug in both adapters to a power source.

Follow the steps below:

1. Switch on the new device and place it beside the old one. To transfer data using the wired method, connect the iPhones. When the Quick Start Screen appears with the option to use an Apple ID to set up the new device, select yes. Press the Continue button to proceed. If the Continue button doesn't appear, check to see if Bluetooth is enabled.
2. Wait for the animated logo to display on your screen then hold your old iPhone over the new one and position it at the centre of the viewfinder. Hold for a message saying, Finish on New iPhone. If the camera on your old iPhone is not working, press the Authenticate Manually tab and follow the instructions.
3. Insert the passcode of old iPhone into the new device.
4. Follow the onscreen steps to configure Face ID or Touch ID on your new device.
5. Select the Transfer from iPhone tab to transfer data from the old iPhone to the new one. For a cable transfer, this icon shows that the devices are connected. You can also transfer customized settings like Apple Pay and Siri from the old iPhone to the new one.
6. Apple watch users can transfer their Apple watch settings to the new iPhone.
7. Ensure the iPhone devices are close to each other and connected to power. The time frame for the transfer process depends on factors such as the amount of data, network speed and so on.

How to activate your iPhone

The device must be connected to a Wi-Fi, a cellular network, or iTunes to activate and set up your iPhone.

Select the preferred Wi-Fi network and enter the password.

As soon as this sign 📶 appears, it means that your Wi-Fi is turned on.

If you're setting up an iPhone (Wi-Fi + Cellular), you might need to insert your SIM card first.

How to install the nano-SIM?
1. Push the SIM tray to eject.
2. Gently remove the tray from the iPhone.
3. Insert the nano-SIM into the tray.
4. Push the tray into the iPhone gradually.

How to manage your cellular service providers?
This part will help you set up your cellular plan the way it suits you. Your settings will determine how iPhone 11 makes use of each cellular service provider.

Go to settings > tap Cellular and follow these instructions;

1. Press the Cellular and pick a service provider.
2. You can change settings such as Cellular Plan Label, Calls, SIM pin code.

If you want to register your phone number for iMessage and Face Time, go to setting, tap iMessage and Face Time and follow the instructions. You can't register more than one number for iMessage and Face Time.

Note the following if you're using Dual SIM;

1. Any incoming call when you're on the other network will automatically go to voicemail. You may not receive a missed call notification. However, this will only happen when the voicemail service is activated.
2. The calling waiting only works if the incoming call is on the same network.

3. Switching conversations from one network to another is not possible. Then, if you must, you may incur charges for your service provider.

Configure your Face ID or Touch ID

It's time to set up your Face ID or Touch ID. These features will allow you to unlock your iPhone with your facial recognition or fingerprint. Press the Continue button or Set Up Later in Settings to proceed.

Setting up the Face ID

When you launch your iPhone 11 for the first time, you will be asked to set up the Face ID. You may choose to set it up later or when you're more comfortable. Please have it in mind that Face ID can only memorize one face. It doesn't matter when you choose to set up the Face ID, and the process is the same. The entire process is easy and fast to set up.

Go to Settings > Face ID & Passcode, enter Password. Then the image below will appear. Just tap on Get Started to start the process.

Position your face for the front camera to capture you. Immediately, the sensor recognizes that there is a face ready to scan, you will hear an interesting background that will let you know that your face is about to be scanned.

On the screen this will display Move your head slowly to complete the circle. Just do a slow neck roll while you hold your iPhone 11. This will help the iPhone 11 to map all the angles and corners on your face. You will also hear interesting animation sounds as you move your face in a circle.

As you keep moving your face, a circle in green color will cover your face.

You will have to go through the process twice. The essence is to ensure that all angles of your face are scanned properly.

When the process is completed, tap the Done tab.

Face ID Options

After setting up the Face ID, you also need to choose when it should function. As a default setting, you must look at the iPhone 11 directly to unlock it. The fact that you have to look at the iPhone directly means that somebody cannot snatch your iPhone and hold it up to your face when you're not paying attention.

If you have any disability or wear sunglasses, just put off the Require Attention for Face ID. You will find this in the Settings > Face ID & the Passcode section.

If Face ID identifies that you are looking at the screen, it will dim the screen or play the message alerts or whatever notifications at a low volume. However, you can put this feature off when you tap the Attention Aware Features.

You can also choose the section you want to use the Face ID to function. For instance, you can turn it off for Apple Pay, third-party apps, App store, etc.

You can set up an alternative appearance. For instance, when you are wearing a hat or a sunglasses. The process is the same as mentioned earlier. Just tap Set up Alternative Appearance.

Although the Face ID is remarkably accurate, there are a few instances that it may struggle to identify your face. If you notice such, you can do the following;

Move a little bit closer to your iPhone.

Take off your sunglasses. The Face ID will not recognize your face if you're putting on a sunglasses that blocks infrared.

Step away from a very bright light.

As you keep using the Face ID, it will also identify your face even if you change your hair style or mustache. It is that accurate. Also, if the Face ID is not sure it's you, it will ask for your passcode to unlock.

Setting up your Touch ID

The first thing you need to do is to set up a passcode for your iPhone. Follow the steps below:

1. Ensure your finger and the Home button on your device are clean and dry
2. Tap Settings > Touch ID & Passcode tab, then insert your preferred passcode
3. Tap Add a Fingerprint and hold the device the same way you would with the Home button
4. Tap the Home Button briefly. Press and hold the Home Button until it vibrates.
5. Lift your finger slowly and make small adjustments as requested.
6. Release your grip on the device. Hold on to the iPhone the same way you would when unlocking it. Tap the Home Button with the outer part of your fingertip and not with the centre area that was scanned.
7. If your device is not scanning a particular finger, try using another.

The Touch ID set up will allow you to unlock your device with your finger. Simply press and hold the Home Button with the finger you used to register with Touch ID.

How to buy items with Touch ID

Do you know that you can use Touch ID to buy items on iTunes Store, Apps, etc. instead of Apple ID password? Follow these step by step instructions;

1. Ensure that iTunes and App Store are switched on. If you are having challenges turning it on, then login with your Apple ID in Settings > iTunes and App Store.
2. Launch the iTunes Store, App Store, or the Apples Books.

3. Tap on any item you want to purchase. A Touch ID prompt will appear.
4. Touch the Home Button to buy an item.

Managing Touch ID settings

Tap Settings > Touch ID & Passcode to set up your Touch ID

1. Turn on the Touch ID or switch it off for Passcode, iTunes & App Store, or Apple Pay.
2. Register at least 5 fingerprints. The pattern may increase the time used for fingerprint recognition a little bit longer.
3. You can rename a fingerprint. Just tap it.
4. To delete a fingerprint, just swipe.
5. If you want to know the fingerprint on the list, touch the Home Button.

To unlock your iPhone, tap the Home Button using Touch ID. Alternatively, if you want to unlock your Touch ID without pressing the Home Button tap Setting > General> Accessibility > Home Button and switch on the Rest Finger to Open.

A passcode

The next step is to set up a six-digit passcode that will assist in protecting your data. To access Face ID, Touch ID, and Apple Pay, you must obtain a passcode. If you want to customize your passcode or no passcode at all, press Passcode Options.

Using passcode with your device

Set up a passcode for additional protection of your data. You can either use a fingerprint or your passcode. Your device will request for a passcode to do the following;

- To switch on or restart your iPhone
- Tap the Home button or swipe upward to unlock your iPhone
- Update your software
- Erase your device

- View or alter the passcode settings
- Install iOS or iPadOS Configuration profiles

Setting up a passcode

1. Visit Setting > Face ID & Passcode
2. Press the Turn Passcode On tab
3. Insert a 6-digit passcode. If you prefer 4 digits, press Passcode Options. You can either insert a custom numeric code or alphanumeric code
4. Insert the passcode again to confirm and activate it.

How to alter your passcode?

Tap Settings > Face ID & Passcode. The following settings and options will appear;

1. **Turn Passcode Off:** Press this tab to switch off the passcode.
2. **Change Passcode:** Insert a new 6-digit passcode. To use a 4-digit passcode, press Passcode Options.
3. **Require Passcode:** Whenever the screen is locked, the default setting will request that you insert your passcode to unlock the device. You can alter the settings if you don't want the passcode requirement immediately.
4. **Allow Access When Locked:** You can activate this option to allow the use of certain features even when the device is locked. Some features that could be allowed are Today View, Siri, Reply with Message, Wallet, etc.
5. **Erase Data:** You can activate this setting if you want your passcode to be deactivated or erased after 10 failed attempts. The advantage is that you don't have to use your PC to restore your device after 10 failed attempts.

How to restore or transfer data?

If you didn't store your data or information on iCloud or iTunes backup, you can transfer your data from the old iPhone to the new one.

Transferring to the iCloud backup to your new iPhone

1. Switch on the new iPhone. Hello will display on the screen. Assuming you have already configured your new iPhone, the configuration must be erased to use these steps. (To erase the device, press Settings > General > Reset > Erase All Content and Settings. This will erase the previous data on the iPhone. As soon as the data is erased, the iPhone will restart automatically.
2. Continue until the Wi-Fi screen appears
3. Press any Wi-Fi network to join. Follow the instructions until the Apps & Data screen appears. Press Restore from iCloud Backup
4. Log in to iCloud using your Apple ID and password
5. Select a backup. To ensure that it is the correct one confirm check the data and size of all backups.
6. If you have purchased iTunes or App Store items with several Apple ID's, you will be required to login into each account. If you have forgotten the passwords, skip the option by pressing I Don't have an Apple ID, or I forgot my Apple ID.
7. Don't disconnect your device until the connection process is concluded. Let the iPhone remain connected to Wi-Fi or plugged into a power source during the entire process. This will allow your pictures, music and other contents that are stored in iCloud to download.

Transferring your iTunes backup to the new iPhone

1. Switch on the new iPhone. A Hello will display on the screen. To continue with these steps, you must erase the previous set up on the new iPhone. (To erase the previous set up, press Settings > General > Reset > Erase All Content Settings. This will erase the previous data on the iPhone. As soon as the data is erased, the iPhone will restart automatically).
2. When Apps & Data appears press Restore from Mac or PC.

3. Connect the new iPhone to the PC that backed up the old device.
4. Launch iTunes or Finder on your PC and choose your device. A pop up requesting you to trust your device may appear.
5. Choose Restore Backup. Select the backup and ensure it is the correct file by checking the date and size.
6. If you are restoring from an encrypted backup, you have to insert your password
7. Don't disconnect your device until the connection process is concluded. Let the iPhone remain connected to Wi-Fi or plugged to power during and after the entire process. This will allow your pictures, music and other contents that are stored in iCloud to download.

Switching from an Android device to iPhone

1. Before you start this process, do the following on your Android device;

- Turn on the Wi-Fi
- Plug the Android and new iPhone to power
- Ensure that the content you are moving is compatible with your iPhone
- To transfer your Chrome bookmarks, ensure that the Chrome on your Android device is up to date.
- When Apps & Data appears on the screen, press Move Data from Android.

2. Launch the Move to iOS app

- Launch the Move to iOS app and press Continue. Go through the T&C. Hit the Agree button and press Next at the top-right side of the Find Your Code screen.

3. Wait a code will appear

- Insert the code on your Android device. Hold on a bit, the Transfer Data screen will appear
- Press Continue on your new iPhone known as Move from Android. Hold on, a 10 digit or 6-digit code will display on

the screen. Peradventure a prompt appears on your Android device that you might be experiencing a bad connection, ignore the prompt.

4. Insert the code
   - Insert the code on your Android device. Hold until Transfer Data is displayed on the screen.
5. Select the content
   - Choose the content that you want to transfer to your new iPhone device and press Next. Do not disconnect when the prompt appears showing that the process has been completed until the loading bar is full. The transfer process may take some time. The amount of content being transferred will determine the timeframe.

6. Setting up your iPhone

   - When the loading bar on your iPhone is full, press Done on your Android device. Tap the Continue button on your new iPhone.

7. Finalizing the process

   - Ensure that all the content you wanted to transfer have been moved
   - Content such as music, books, and PDFs are better moved manually

Log in with your Apple ID

Insert your Apple ID and password. If you can't remember the password, press Forgot password or don't have an Apple ID? icon. This will let you recover the forgotten or Apple ID. If you used two different Apple IDs, press the Use different Apple IDs for iCloud and iTunes?

A verification code will be sent to your previous device.

Management of Apple ID

Your Apple ID is like the Pass you need to do almost everything on your iPhone 11. However, this is not peculiar to just the iPhone 11, other models also make use of an Apple ID. If you don't have an Apple ID, you can't store content on iCloud, purchase contents from iTunes Store, App Store, etc. So you see how important an Apple ID is?

How to sign in with your Apple ID?

Assuming you didn't sign in during setup, follow these instructions;

1. Settings > Click Sign in > Insert your Apple ID and password
2. You don't have to worry if you forgot your password, just go to Recover Apple ID website (link).

How to change your Apple ID settings?

Go to iPhone Settings (enter your name) and do any of the following;

1. Update your contact information.
2. Change password.
3. Manage family sharing.

The iCloud helps you store your photos, videos, documents, music and so on securely. It also helps you share pictures, locations, music and lots more to your loved ones. Do you know that you can use the iCloud to find your iPhone when it's lost? Just keep reading you will find out about this shortly.

iCloud also gives you a free email account and 5 GB to store your mail, pictures, videos, etc. You can also upgrade your iCloud Storage space from your iPhone.

Please note that you may not have access to all the features on iCloud if you reside in some regions. Also, the iCloud features may vary from one region to another.

How to change your iCloud settings?

Go to Settings > (your name) > iCloud, you can do any of the following;

- Check your iCloud memory
- Upgrade your iCloud memory
- Turn on the features you need

Features of the iCloud

The iCloud is a unique feature that you can only find on Apple's iPhone. Here are features of iCloud that will interest you;

- You can use the iCloud to update your messages, mail, contacts, calendars, photos, videos, music, app, books, contents, passwords and credit cards.
- Share images and videos with your friends.
- You can locate iOS, Apple watch, or Mac devices that belong to you or a friend.
- Back up your contents.
- Share your location with your friends and family.

Please note that enabling iCloud for apps like music, photos, and contacts will stop you from using iTunes to synchronize them to your PC.

Activate automatic updates and set up additional features

Here you can allow information sharing with app developers and automatic iPhone device updates.

Setting up Siri

To set up Siri and activate other features, your iPhone device will request that you say a few words so that Siri will get familiar with your voice.

If you logged in with your Apple ID, then follow the instructions to activate Apple Pay iCloud Keychain.

How to add a card on your device

1. Go to Wallet and the press ⊕ button
2. Follow the instructions that will pop up to add a new card. You can also add the cards that you are using or removed from the old iPhone. Insert the security code. You may be asked to download an app from your bank or card issuer to add a card to your wallet. iPhone users in China mainland may have to create a 6-digit passcode.
3. Press the Next button to continue. The bank or card issuer will verify your details and let you know if you can use the card with Apple pay. The card issuer or bank may request additional details if the need arises. Then input the new details, go to Wallet and press the card.
4. Press Next after the bank or card issuers verification. You can now begin using Apple Pay with your device.

iCloud Keychain

Types of information stored by iCloud

iCloud Keychain primarily stores information about credit card numbers and expiration dates. It does not store or autofill the security code or passwords. Other details such as Wi-Fi passwords, usernames, internet accounts and so on are not stored by iCloud.

Can I turn off iCloud? - What happens when I do?

You can turn off iCloud Keychain. However, when you turn it off, you will be asked if you want to store or delete the passwords and credit card details that are stored on your device. If you choose to delete the information, all Keychain data will be removed from your device and iCloud servers.

How to turn on iCloud Keychain on your iPhone

1. Press Settings, tap [your name], then tap iCloud
2. Press Keychain
3. Slide to switch on iCloud Keychain

4. If you select Approve Later when you are logging in to Apple ID, you must insert the previous passcode you used on your old device. If you have forgotten the passcode, reset the end-to-end encryption when prompted.

How to set up Screen Time and other display options

If you want to monitor how much time you are spending on your iPhone, then go to Screen Time. You can set daily time limits for each app on your device. If your iPhone supports True Tone, you can turn it on after you have set up Screen Time. To adjust the size of the icons and text that appear on your home screen, use Display Zoom.

Finishing up

Press the Get Started button to start using your device.

Basics

Learn the controls on the iPhone

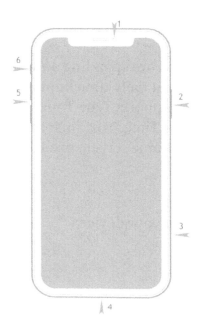 

1. Front-facing cameras

2. Side button

3. SIM tray

4. Lightning connector

5. Volume buttons

6. Ring/Silent switch

7. Rear cameras

8. Flash

Learn basic gestures to interact with iPhone 11

The iPhone 11 has some simple gestures that will help you control the device and use all apps effectively.

 Tap - touch your finger lightly on the screen

 Press - touch and hold

 Swipe - move your finger across the screen swiftly

 Open Camera - swipe left

See Today View - swipe right

See earlier notification - swipe up from the center

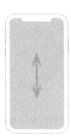

Scroll - move your finger across the screen without removing it

Zoom - place two of your fingers close to each other on the screen of the iPhone 11. If you want to zoom in spread them apart, then to zoom out move them towards each other. Another way to zoom is to tap the screen. You can zoom in double tapping and also do the same to zoom out

Go Home - move your finger from the bottom of the screen to go back to the Home screen

To unlock then swipe up from the bottom of the Lock screen

To see notifications, like phone calls, reminders and messages - swipe down from the top of your screen

Quickly access controls - move your fingers from the top right hand side of the screen to access the Control Center. If you want to add or remove some items, Go to Settings > Control Center > Customize Control

Switch between recent apps - move your finger from the bottom of the screen pause at the middle to display the App Switcher

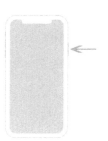

Ask Siri - press and hold the Side button and make your request. Remove your hands when you're done with your request

To put your iPhone to sleep, press the side button.

To turn on, press and hold the side button until the Apple Logo appears

Search - to quickly find anything on your device and on the web, swipe down from the middle of the screen

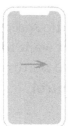

Find widgets - to see information from apps you've added to widgets, swipe right from the Home or Lock screen

Use Apple Pay - tap the Side button twice to show your default credit card. Look at the iPhone 11 directly to authenticate with Face ID

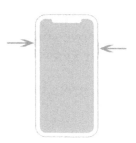

Take a Screenshot - press the Side button and volume up at the same time

Use Accessibility Shortcut - tap the Side button three time swiftly

Make an emergency call - this feature is available in other regions except India. Press and hold the Side button and the volume button until the sliders display, then drag Emergency SOS

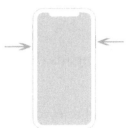

Turn off - press and hold the side and volume button until the slider displays. Then move the top slider to turn it off. You can also choose to Go to Settings > General > Shut Down

Force restart - press and release the volume up button, then do the same with the Side button and volume down button. Finally, press and hold the Side button until the Apple logo displays

Check out the meaning of status icons on iPhone 11

The icon that display in the status bar helps you know the app is turned on or off.

Cell signal – This signal informs you how strong or weak the strength of your cellular service is. If there is no network signal, No Service will display in place of the cellular signal

Dual cell signals – The first cellular signal bar shows the strength of the first line on your iPhone while the lower signal bar is on the second line

Airplane mode – If you see this sign, it shows that the Airplane mode is activated. This means that you can't make or receive calls or perform any wireless functions

LTE	This sign indicates that your LTE network is available. This feature is not available all the regions
4G	This signal shows that 4G UMTS network is available. However, this is not available in some regions
3G	This signal indicates that you can access 3G UMTS (GSM) network
E	EDGE – If this feature appears, then it means that EDGE network is available
5G E	**5G** E Your carrier's 5G E network is available, and iPhone can connect to the Internet over that network (not available in all regions)
GPRS	The iPhone 11 can connect to the GPRS
Wi-Fi	If the Wi-Fi call is activated, you can make calls with your iPhone 11
🛜	This signal means that your Wi-Fi is connected
⊘	This sign shows that your Personal Hotspot is connected to another device for use
9:41	Personal Hotspot Indicator - A blue bubble or bar indicates iPhone is either providing a Personal Hotspot or Screen Mirroring, or an app is actively using your location
9:41	Call Indicator - A green bubble or bar indicates iPhone is on a call
9:41	Recording Indicator - A red bubble or bar indicates iPhone is either recording sound or recording your screen

CarPlay iPhone is connected to CarPlay

If this signal appears, it means that your iPhone 11 is syncing with iTunes

It shows that network activities are turned on. Some third-party app may also use this signal to show that it is active

It means that the Call Forwarding is turned on

It shows that you are connected to a VPN network

This signal shows that software RTT/TTY is turned on

It means that your iPhone 11 is locked

Means that Do not disturb is turned on

Shows that the iPhone screen is locked in portrait orientation

As soon as you see this, it means that Location Service is being used

It shows that an alarm is turned on

It indicates that a Bluetooth headphone is turned and paired to your iPhone 11

It displays the battery level of a Bluetooth device paired with your iPhone 11

It lets you know the battery level or charging status of the iPhone 11. If yellow appears, it means that Low Power Mode is on

Battery Charging - Shows the iPhone battery is charging

How to use the iPhone Home screen and open apps?

The Home screen of any phone including the iPhone 11 displays all the apps on the device. Follow the instructions below;

1. Swipe up from the bottom edge of the iPhone 11 screen
2. Move left or right to go through apps on your Home screen pages
3. If you want to open an app, tap it
4. To go back to the Home screen, swipe up from the bottom edge

Change your iPhone Settings

The Settings of the iPhone 11 helps you to configure and customize the device. You can choose your preferred language, sounds, notification, etc.

You can do the following through the Settings;

Set the date and time of your iPhone 11

The default time of the iPhone is set based on your location. However, you can change it if they are not correct.

Go to Settings > General > Date and Time.

You can also do any of the following;

- Set Automatically: This option allows the iPhone 11 to set the time and date as provided by your network. However, in some regions, some networks don't support automatically setting the time and date of your iPhone.
- 24-Hour Time: This feature is not available in all regions.

Set language and region
To carry out this function, do the following;

1. Go to Settings > General > Language and Region.

You can also set the following;

- The language of the iPhone
- Region
- The Calendar format
- The temperature unit
2. If you want to add a keyboard for another language, go to Settings > General > Keyboard > Keyboards.

How to change the name of your iPhone 11?
Tap Settings > General > About > Name.

Touch , insert the name of your choice and press Done.

Setting up an email, contact and calendar accounts
The iPhone 11 works with Microsoft Exchange and other familiar Internet – based mail.

Tap to Settings > Passwords & Accounts > Add Account.

Adding an email account requires that you tap any service provider. E.g. Google, Yahoo, etc.

How to change other settings?
Tap Settings > swipe downwards > insert a term e.g. alert, password, music etc.

How to change or lock the iPhone 11 screen orientation?

Most apps on the iPhone 11 have a different layout when the device is in landscape orientation. Such apps are Mail, Message, and Photos.

Please **note** that these different layouts are not accessible when you Zoom in.

Unlocking or locking the screen orientation

If you don't want the screen orientation to change when the iPhone rotates, lock the screen orientation. Simply launch the Control Center and touch ⟳.

How to change the wallpaper on your iPhone?

Select the image you want as your wallpaper for the Lock screen or Home screen. You can use a dynamic or still image.

Tap Settings > Wallpaper > Select a New Wallpaper.

You can also do any of the following;

- Select any preset image from a group at the top of the screen
- Choose any of your pictures from your album or photo

If you want to reposition the photo you selected, double click the screen to zoom in or out. Move the photo with your finger to reposition it.

Press Set, then select from any of the following where the wallpaper should display.

- Set Lock screen
- Set Home screen
- Set as both

Do you know that you can also change the viewing angle of your screen? Simply press Perspective after you have selected a new wallpaper.

Simply tap Settings > Wallpaper > press the image for the Lock screen or Home screen > touch Perspective.

How to activate or deactivate Dark Mode

For a low-light environment, turn on the Dark Mode function. The iPhone screen will appear dark for better vision. For instance, if you are reading while in bed, you can turn on the Dark Mode. The light from your device will not affect other people in the room.

1. Go to Control Center > press and hold ☼ > touch ◐ to switch on or off Dark Mode

2. Tap Settings ⚙ > press Display & Brightness > tap Dark to activate Dark Mode. To turn it off, tap Light.

Automatic Programming to turn on or off Dark Mode

1. Tap Settings ⚙ > then press Display & Brightness
2. Tap Automatic > then press Options
3. Choose Sunset to Sunrise or Custom Schedule.

If you select Custom to Sunrise press the options available to program the time you want Dark Mode to be turned on or off.

On the other hand, if you choose Sunset to Sunrise, then your device will determine nighttime through your clock and geographical location.

How to increase or reduce the iPhone 11 screen brightness and color?

When the iPhone 11 brightness is reduced, it helps your battery last longer. You can adjust the brightness manually.

Tap Control Center and drag ☼

Tap Settings > Display and Brightness > slider down or up to reduce or increase.

To adjust the screen brightness automatically

- Tap Settings > General > Accessibilty
- Press Display Accomodation > switch on Auto Brightness.

How to amplify the iPhone 11 screen with Display Zoom?

To magnify what's displayed on your screen, do the following;

- Tap Settings > Display and Brightness
- Press View
- Select Zoomed and press Set.

Switch on and use Reachability

- Tap Settings > General > Accessibility > Reachability.
- To get the top of the screen, Swipe down to the bottom edge of the screen.

If you want to reset the screen, press the top of the screen.

Adjusting volume on your iPhone 11

You can adjust the volume of the iPhone via the Volume button. You can find it on the side of the device. Siri is also there to help. Just ask Siri to either reduce or increase the volume it will be done immediately.

Adjusting volume on your iPhone 11 in Control Center.

Another way to adjust your iPhone 11 volume is through the Control center.

Launch Control Center > drag ◀)).

When the device is in ring mode, it plays every sound. However, in silent mode, the iPhone doesn't produce any sound or alert. The iPhone will vibrate even it's in silent mode.

Note: clock alarms and other apps like Music will play sounds even when the iPhone 11 is on silent mode.

How to adjust iPhone 11 sound and vibrations?

You can adjust or change the sounds iPhone plays when you get a call, email, reminder, and other notifications.

Setting sound and vibration options

- Tap Settings > Sounds and Haptics
- Drag the slider either above Ringers and Alert to adjust the volume for all sounds
- To adjust the vibration pattern and tones, press the type of sound you want; e.g. ringtone or text tone.

Note: If the iPhone doesn't make any sound when you receive incoming calls, go to the Control Center and check if Do Not Disturb is turned on. If you see 🌙 turned on, tap it to put it off.

Notifications

Notifications will keep you posted on what's new. You can also customize your notifications to view what's important to you.

You will receive all the notifications as soon as they arrive. Assuming, you don't open it, all notifications will be saved. To view all the notifications, swipe down from top of the screen. To close the Notification, swipe up.

When the notifications are so many, they are grouped by the app. That way, it will be easier to view and manage. If the notification is grouped, it will display as small stacks and the most current notification will appear on top.

Do any of the following;

- You can expand the group notifications to view them individually.
- Touch the notification to view it.
- If you want to respond to the notification, swipe to the right and open it.

You can either dismiss or clear your notifications. There are ways to manage your notifications;

- When you are using another app and receive a notification, swipe down to view and swipe up to dismiss.
- To clear your notifications, swipe to the left-hand side > press clear or clear all.
- To send notifications to the Notification Center, swipe to the left.
- Whenever you want to turn off notification for an app, swipe to the left > touch Manage > press to turn off.

To clear all your notifications in the Notification Center, touch .

When an app has not been used for a long time, Siri often suggests that that the app is turned off.

Tap Settings > Notifications > Siri Suggestions > turn off.

DND

Set up Do Not Disturb
This function quickly silence your iPhone if you don't want to receive calls or notifications. You can ask Siri to turn on Do Not Disturb.

- Go to Control Center > touch 🌙.
- To turn it off also press 🌙.

How to turn on Do Not Disturb while Driving?
Turning on Do Not Disturb while Driving helps you to drive safely without any distraction. This helps you silence messages and notification. Siri will help you read the replies aloud so that you won't have to look at the iPhone. You will only receive calls when the car Bluetooth system is turned on.

- Tap Settings > Do Not Disturb.

- Move down > press Activate.

You can do any of the following;

- Turn on Do Not Disturb while driving to detect when you're driving automatically. This means that Do Not Disturb while driving will be turned on as soon as it detects that you are driving.
- Turn it on when Connected to Car Bluetooth.
- You can also turn it on manually.

Note: If CarPlay is activated, Do Not Disturb while driving will not work.

Sending an auto-reply that you are driving

When activate Do Not Disturb while driving, it will auto-reply any message sent to you.

- Tap Settings > Do Not Disturb > Auto-Reply To.

You can do any of the following;

- No One: Turn off auto-reply.
- Recent: The iPhone will auto-reply to anyone who you sent a message previously.
- Favorite: Your device will send an auto-reply to your favorite group on your iPhone.

Assuming you receive a message with the heading Urgent, the remaining texts will go to the reminder drive.

If you want to enjoy a bedtime without any interference, set Do Not Disturb during Bedtime. It will reduce the display, reduce calls, all through the night until the morning.

How to type and edit text?
There are so many apps that require the use of text. Some of them are Contacts, Messages, Notes, Mail, etc.

You can do the following while inserting text;

- Press Shift and touch the letter to use Uppercase letters.
- Tap the Shift key twice swiftly to turn on Caps Lock.
- Press 123 to enter numbers or Symbols such as $\#+=$.
- To Undo the last edit, shake the device and press Undo.
- To use emoji, touch ☺ or ⊕.
- To use accented letters or other characters, press and hold the key.

Correct spelling

If your text is underlined in red, it means that the spelling is wrong.

Touch the underlined word to view the correct spelling or suggestions.

Touch the suggestion to replace the underlined word.

Type with one hand

To use one hand to type your text, move the keys closer to your thumb.

Press and hold ☺ or ⊕.

Slide and select one of the keyboard layouts.

Typing options

If you don't want a spelling check to be on, you can turn it off.

Press and hold ☺ or ⊕ > move to Keyboard Settings.

Typing options that you can turn on or off are Auto-Capitalization, Auto-Correction, etc.

How to choose a text?

Touch and Hold the text > allow the magnifying glass to show > drag to place an insertion point.

Use the keyboard as a trackpad

Press and hold the Space bar until the color of the keyboard becomes light gray.

Slide the insertion point around the keyboard.

You can carry out any of the following as you type a text;

You can accept a suggested word or emoji.

Reject a suggestion by touching the original text.

How to turn off predictive text?

Press and hold ☺ or ⊕ .

Go to the Keyboard Setting and switch off Predictive.

Inasmuch as you turn off the Prediction, the iPhone 11 will still provide suggestions of misspelled text. You can either accept or decline. If the rejection is consistent, iPhone 11 will stop suggesting.

Dictate a text for the iPhone

If you don't want to type a text, you can detect it. However, this feature may not be available in all regions.

Tap Settings > General > Keyboard.>Turn on or off Enable Dictation.

Press 🎤 in the onscreen keyboard.

Read out the text.

When you are through, press ⌨.

How to add punctuation to a text?

While you are dictating the text, you also have to read out the punctuation. For instance, Hello Alice comma the check is in the your mail exclamation mark full stop. Some of the punctuation and formatting command;

- Quote ... end quote
- New line
- Cap – to capitalize the next word.
- Smiley – to insert :-)
- Frowny – to insert :-(

Customize and use Control Center

When you go to Control Center, it will give you access to Do Not Disturb, flashlight, etc.

- Open Control Center > tap the top-left group of controls > press  > AirDrop options.
- Open Control Center > tap 📷 to take a selfie.
- Open Control Center > press 📶 to reconnect.
- If you want to see the name of the Wi-Fi network, tap 📶
- To switch off Wi-Fi tap Settings > Wi-Fi. (Switch on Wi-Fi in the Control Center and press 📶.)
- To connect to Bluetooth open Control Center > press ✱.
- Tap Settings > Control Center > turn off Access Within Apps.
- If you choose to customize controls, tap Settings > Control Center > Customize Controls. Tap ≡ next to a control move it to a new position.

Adding more controls: You can also add or remove controls from the Control Centre. Just go to Settings > Control Centre > Customize Controls and then select the controls you will prefer.

Reorganize controls: You can rearrange the new controls. Just tap and hold the 3-bar icon on the right side of the control you added to move it. Move it to whatever position you want.

Expanding controls: You can make some controls full screen by simply pressing on the control for a few seconds.

Turn on personal hotspot: The default setting of the connectivity control has just 4 options. If you press and hold for a few seconds, it will have a full-screen control with an additional 2 options. Press the personal hotspot button to turn it on.

Turning on-screen recording: Another option that was included in 2018 to the Control Centre is Screen Recording. After you have added this option, launch Control Centre > tap the button that resembles a solid white circle inside a thin white ring. This will activate the recording of whatever action that happens on your screen. Tap the control button when you are through. The video will be stored to the Photo app instantly.

Adjusting flashlight or torch brightness: If you want to use your flashlight as a torch, go to Control Centre > then press the torch icon. To change the level of brightness, touch and hold the icon and then move the full-screen slider that appeared.

Switching where to play audio: from Another new feature is the ability to change where audio is playing. Tap and hold the music control for a few seconds. Available devices where you can play your music through will pop-up. You can play it through your earphones, Bluetooth speaker, Apple TV, etc.

Setting a quick timer: Press and hold the timer icon and slide it up or down to set your timer.

Accessing Home Kit devices: Launch the Control Center > press the small icon that is like a house to access Home Kit devices.

Lock Screen

How to launch your camera from the lock screen: Tap the bottom on the right corner of the lock screen to launch the camera app.

Turn on your torch: Press the lock screen button to turn on the torch.

Tap to wake: To wake up your device, tap the screen gently. The device will light up and your lock screen will appear.

Raise your iPhone to wake up: Just lift the device from where you kept it and all the notifications will show thereby leaving the standby mode. To switch on or off this feature tap Settings > Display & Brightness > then slide Raise to wake to put it on or off.

Notification Center: Normally, notifications usually pop up on your lock screen. To read the older notifications earlier, swipe up on the centre of the lock screen. Then the Notification Center will collate your previous notifications. Don't start from the button that is too low. You may end up unlocking your device and go to the home screen.

Clearing notifications: Since the Notification Centre is still on the screen, then tap X button at the corner.

Accessing Today View widgets on the lock screen: Just swipe from the left hand on the lock screen.

Unlocking your device while the lock screen is active: This feature is interesting if your Face ID has been set up. Simply pick up the device and the padlock icon at the topmost part of your screen will you show you that it is unlocking. While this is going on, you will not be allowed to use your apps until you swipe up.

Quick Reply: If you want to respond to a notification without opening the app, pull down the notification to show the options available. Another way is to touch and hold the notification and press Reply then enter your response.

How to remove individual or grouped notifications: just swipe from the right to the left side of the screen and press Clear or Clear all.

Open and organize Today View

Today View helps you get an information from favorite apps. You can view today headlines, calendar, etc.

- Tap Today View > press Edit below the screen.
- If you want to remove widgets, press ⊕ or ⊖ .
- If you want to adjust the pattern of the widgets in Today View, tap ≡ > move it to a new position. Tap Settings > Face ID & Passcode > Insert your passcode >Switch on Today View.

Screen Time

You can set how the allowances and screen time are used. Screen Time will provide a summary of how long you spend on each app on your iPhone. It will also provide information about the apps that send you notifications regularly. This information will assist you to set limits for some apps and websites.

Open your Screen Time summary

As soon as you set up the Screen Time, it will prepare a summary of how you use your iPhone 11. It will give you an insight into how you use the apps. If you want to see your Screen Time summary, tap Settings > Screen Time > insert the name of your device. The summary will contain the following;

- The amount of time you spend on each app.
- The breakdown of how you use the app by the time each day.
- The time you spent on each app and the app that you used above the time limit.
- A summary of all the notifications you get.
- Which app you use frequently.

Setup Screen Time for yourself

This will afford you the opportunity to set allowances and limits for each app. Here is how to set it up;

- Tap Settings > Screen Time.
- Press Turn On Screen Time > touch Continue > press This is My iPhone.

You can carry out any of the following:

- You can set up the start and end times by turning on Downtime.
- Press App Limits > Add Limit > choose one or more categories.
- Press Always Allowed > press ⊕ or ⊖ close to the app to either include it or remove it.

Setting up parental control on your kid's iPhone

The Content & Privacy Restrictions in Screen Time helps you limit the types of apps and other features your child can use on their device. This will also help you limit the types of contents and downloads that your child can access.

How to set up content and privacy restrictions

- Go to Settings and press Screen Time
- Press the Continue tab > select This is My [device] or This My Child's [device].
- If you don't want any family member to change your settings, press Use Screen Time Passcode to generate a passcode. Insert the passcode again to confirm.
- Follow all the instructions until Parent Passcode appears. Insert a passcode, then re-enter it to confirm.
- Press Content & Privacy Restrictions. Insert the passcode and then switch on the Content & Privacy.

Note: Don't use the same passcode you use to unlock your iPhone. If you want to alter or remove the passcode on your child's device, hit Settings > Screen Time > [your child's name] > press Change Screen Time Passcode or Turn off Screen Time passcode. Verify the alteration with Face ID, Touch ID or your device passcode.

- With this setup, you can limit what your child can install or delete. Tap Settings > Screen Time > Content & Privacy Restrictions (insert your passcode if it is required) > iTunes & App Store Purchases > Choose a setting and activate Don't allow.
- Restricting the use of built-in apps is also possible. If you switch off an app or feature, it doesn't delete it automatically. The app or feature will only be hidden from the Home Screen. To restrict apps, go to Settings > Screen Time > Content & Privacy Restrictions (insert your Screen Time passcode) > tap Allowed apps > then choose the apps you permit.
- You can also limit the playback music, movies, or TV shows. With the ratings, you can also configure what contents your child should listen to or watch. Tap Settings > Screen Time > Content & Privacy Restrictions > Select the settings you prefer for each feature or setting under Allowed Store Content.

- The iOS automatically screens web content that can be accessed on safari and other apps. You can include websites that you want to be blocked or restrict access to only approved sites. Tap Settings > Screen Time > Content & Privacy Restrictions (insert Screen Time passcode) > Content Restrictions > Web Content > Select Unrestricted Access, Limit Adult Websites or Allowed Websites Only.
- Limit web search on Siri
- Restrict Game Center

The Privacy setting aims to enable you to control the apps and features that can be accessed on the device. For instance, you can permit a social-networking site to access your camera. Tap Settings > Screen Time > Content & Privacy Restrictions (insert your passcode if it is requested) > Privacy > select the settings you would like to limit access to.

Setting up communication limits on a family members iPhone

You can block incoming and outgoing phone calls on a family member's iPhone. You can also block FaceTime calls and messages. This restriction can be for a certain period or at all times.

1. Switch on Contacts in iCloud on your family members iPhone, tap Settings > [child's names] > iCloud, put on Contacts.
   However, the only way you can manage their communications is when they make use of Contacts in iCloud.
2. Go to Settings > Screen Time on the family members iPhone
3. To put on Screen Time press, Turn on Screen Time > hit the Continue button, then touch This is My Child's iPhone.
4. To limit certain communications hit the following options;
- Limit communication at any time
- Limit communication during downtime
- Manage a child's contacts

- Allow contact editing.

Assuming someone is blocked from communicating with your family member tries calling or texting, it will not go through. Likewise, if your family member tries to communicate with the number that is blocked it will not also go through.

Charging and monitoring the iPhone battery

Charge the battery

If you want to charge the battery of your device, do any of the below;

- Plug your device to a power source with the Lightning to USB cable and USB adapter
- Plug your device to a PC using the USB cable
- If the PC is not switched on, it may drain your device battery.

  This icon ⚡ indicates that your iPhone is charging.
- If you are using a Qi-certified charger, make sure the device faces up.
- Don't plug your iPhone to a keyboard unless it has a power USB port.
- To gauge the level of your battery check the upper- right side

  of the screen. 🔋 If the iPhone is synced or used while charging, it takes longer to get a full battery.

If your iPhone battery is low on power, an image that shows the depleted battery will appear on your screen. This means that the battery needs to be charged before using it. Meanwhile, when the battery is very low on power, the battery icon will display a blank image for at least two minutes then the low-battery image will appear.

Warning: If the Lightning connector of your device is wet or stained with liquid, don't connect it to your iPhone.

If you want to view the percentage of your battery on your status bar, Swipe downward from the top-right side of the device.

How to switch on the Low Power Mode

If you activate the Low Power Mode the life span of your battery charge will increase. You can turn it on when you are running on a low battery.

1. Tap Settings ⚙ > Battery
2. Switch on Low Power Mode

When the Low Power Mode is turned on, it reduces background activities. It will limit your iPhone to performing an important task such as making and receiving calls, emails, messages, browsing the internet and so on.

NOTE: If the Low Power Mode was activated automatically by your device, it will revert to normal power mode when the battery has charged to 80%. You may notice that some tasks may be slower when the Low Power Mode is activated.

History of battery usage

Tap Settings ⚙ > Battery.

You can view your battery usage information for the last 24 hours and the last 10 days.

- **Insight and suggestions**: This will provide an insight into how your device energy is consumed. Suggestions on how to reduce the amount of energy consumed will also be provided.
- **Last Charge Level**: Shows you the last time your battery was fully charged and the time the charger was disconnected from the power outlet.
- **Battery Level graph (last 24 hrs.)**: Displays the battery level, and the periods when your iPhone battery was low on energy. It also indicates when the battery was in Low Power Mode.

- **Battery Usage graph (last 24 hrs.)**: Displays the percentage of the battery used daily
- **Activity graph**: Displays all the activity that has happened over a long time. The graph is split between when the screen was turned on or off.
- **Screen On and Screen Off**: Displays the entire activity of a particular timeframe.
- **Battery Usage by App**: Displays the percentage of the battery used by each app within a particular timeframe.
- **Activity by App**: Displays the amount of time an app was used.

Note: To view battery information about the exact hour or day it was used, touch the time interval on the graph.

View your battery's health

1. Tap Settings > Battery
2. Touch Battery Health

You can monitor your battery's peak performance, capacity or whether it needs servicing on your iPhone.

It is common knowledge that after a period of time the performance of rechargeable batteries often drops. You can visit an Apple Authorized Service Provider for a battery replacement.

Optimize device charging time

If you want to slow down the rate of your battery's ageing, then reduce the time taken to fully charged.

1. Touch Settings > Battery > Battery Health
2. Switch on Optimized Battery Charging.

Siri

Siri is a voice assistant. Ask Siri to translate a phrase, calculate, set a timer, find a location, about the weather, and more. Siri can make calls, send mails, read message etc.

Note: To use Siri, iPhone must be connected to the Internet.

For set up Siri go to Settings > Siri & Search > turn on

- Listen for Hey Siri for summon Siri with voice
- Press Side button for Siri for summon Siri by press and hold Side button.

Tell Siri who you are!

You can let Siri know a little bit about yourself. You can disclose information such as your home and office address, your relationships. This will help you get personalized services from Siri. For instance, you can ask Siri to send a message to your wife or FaceTime.

Setting up Siri

1. Tap Contacts and insert all your contact details.

2. Press Settings > Siri & Search > My information > then enter your name.

Teach Siri how to pronounce your name

You can simply say Hi Siri, learn to pronounce my name.

Let Siri know about your relationship

You can say Hi Siri, Blessing Gates is my wife or Hi Siri, Constance John is my mom.

Creating Siri Shortcuts on iPhone

There are apps that help you create shortcuts things you do regularly. You can tell Siri to do the activities for you.

- **Add a shortcut:** Touch Add to Siri when the app suggests a shortcut. Follow the steps on the screen to record a phrase of your choice that will perform the shortcut.
- **Use the shortcut:** Open Siri, and then say the phrase for the shortcut.

Depending on the apps you use frequently, Siri also makes suggestions about shortcuts on the Lock screen and when to begin a search.

To switch off shortcut suggestions for an app, Tap Settings > Siri & Search > Press the app > Switch of Suggest Shortcuts.

What you need to know about Siri Suggestions on your Device

Siri offers suggestions about what it feels you should do next. It may remind you about an email you need to send or based on your schedule, activity that you ought to carry out. Siri can help you do the following activities;

- **Glance at the Lock screen or Begin a search:** Siri observes your routine and based on these makes suggestions about things it feels you need to do. For instance, if you order pizza every morning by 7:00 am, Siri may suggest or remind you to order pizza a few minutes before you normally do.
- **Create email and events:** Siri may make suggestions about people you need to add to your email list or calendar.
- **Receive calls:** Assuming you receive a call from an unknown number, Siri will let you know who is calling based on your phone numbers on your emails.
- **Leave for an event:** Siri assesses the traffic situation and informs you the best time to leave for an event. However, your calendar event must include the location.
- **See your Flight status:** Assuming you have a boarding pass in your mailbox, Siri will inform you about the flight status in maps.

- *Type:* when you insert a text, Siri may suggest the name of movies or places that you viewed on your device some moments back. For instance, if you tell your wife that you are on your way home, Siri will suggest the estimated time of arrival.
- *Search in Safari:* Siri makes suggestions for websites that you may want to search or phrases too- especially those you searched recently.
- *Confirm an appointment or book a flight on a travel site:* Siri may ask you if you want to include it to your calendar.
- *Read News stories:* After observing your routine, Siri may suggest news sites to visit.

To switch off Siri, Tap Settings 	 > Siri & Search, Switch any of the following:

- Suggestions in Search
- Suggestions in Lookup
- Suggestions on Lock Screen

You can also turn off Siri for a particular app. Press the app > tap turn off Show Siri Suggestions.

Changing Siri Settings

Tap Settings 	 > Siri & Search > then can make any of the following changes;

- **Change the voice for Siri:** (this option is not available for all languages) Press Siri Voice > select a male or female voice for Siri or you can change their accent.
- **Stop Siri from responding to the voice command Hi Siri:** Tap turns off Listen for "Hi Siri.
- **Stop Siri from responding to slide or Home button:** tap Hone for Siri.

- **Remove or alter the language Siri should respond to:** press Language.
- **Reduce the voice feedback you get from Siri:** To reduce the voice feedback from Siri, press Voice Feedback then select from the options the available.
- **Stop access to Siri if the iPhone is locked:** Switch off Allow Siri When Locked.
- Adjust the volume of Siri Voice

Try ask Siri something like:

Say Hey Siri and say

- Turn up the volume
- Turn on Do Not Disturb

Press and hold Side button and ask

- How's the weather today?
- What's 15 times 5?
- Set up a meeting with Alice at 10
- What's on my calendar for Monday?
- What time is it?
- What time is it in Bangkok?
- Wake me up tomorrow at 7 a.m.
- What's my sister's work address? (if you created your sister contact)

Hey Siri, what can you do?

Note: If you don't want your iPhone to respond to "Hi Siri Place your device face down or tap Settings > Siri & Search > switch off Listen for Hi Siri

Siri is programed to secure your information and you can choose what you want to share. To find out more, tap Settings > About Ask Siri & Privacy.

See what Siri can do!

You can use Siri to do the following;

- Get answers to questions: You can get details about a particular sport, get answers to mathematical calculations, or search the web, etc. You can ask Siri question like Hi Siri, what was the outcome of Adesanya v. Romero fight? or Hi Siri, what is the shape of the earth?
- If Siri puts up a web link, touch it to view it in Safari.
- Perform tasks with apps on the iPhone: You can Siri to control apps. For instance, if you want to create an event in Calendar, just say Hi Siri, arrange a meeting with Chizi at 10 am, or you can say Hi Siri, include shoes to my shopping list.
- If the onscreen response from Siri has buttons or controls, touch them to view their content.
- Translate languages: just say, Hi Siri, how do I say come in Chinese.
- Tune to your favourite radio station: Just say "Hi Siri, play Coolfm 95.9 or Hi Siri, tune to Wave FM 106.90".

Listen to Air pods

You can listen and respond to messages with Air Pods. If your iPhone is locked, and your iPhone is connected to it, if a message pops into your iPhone, Siri will read the message to your hearing.

If you don't want Siri to read your message, do the following;

1. Remove your Air Pods
2. Just say Stop or Cancel.

If you want reply to message via Siri, just say Reply that's good news.

Siri always repeats what you say and then requests your confirmation before it forwards your reply. If you want Siri to send

your reply without requesting your confirmation tap Settings >

Siri & search > announce Messages, select Reply without Confirmation.

Note: In case you didn't switch on Announce Messages when you set up your Air Pods. Tap Settings > Siri & Search > Announce Messages, switch on Announce Messages with Siri.

Siri can show you examples if you want. Just say Hi Siri, what can you do? or simply touch ❓ when you launch Siri.

Family Sharing

The Family Sharing feature allows up to 6 family members to share some of the amazing features on your iPhone. You can share iTunes Store, App Store, and Apple Books purchases. The others are Apple Music family membership, Apple News+ Subscription, Apple TV channels subscriptions, iCloud storage plan and such more without sharing accounts.

If you want to use the Family Sharing feature, a member of the family (the organizer) must be an adult. The organizer will select features for the family to share and then invite 5 members of the family to join. As soon as 5 family members join, Family Sharing will be set up on their devices instantly.

The organizer (you) have to sign in with your Apple ID and also confirm the Apple ID you used for the iTunes Store, App Store and Apple Books. The Family Share feature doesn't allow anyone to belong to more than one family group at a time.

Note: You can also activate Screen Time for each family member via Family Sharing or individually on their iPhones.

Activating Family Sharing

1. Tap Settings ⚙ > [your name] > tap Set Up Family Sharing
2. Touch the features you would like to share with other family members:

- Purchase Sharing
- iCloud Storage
- Location Sharing
- Screen Time
- Apple Music
- Apple TV+
- TV channels
- Apple Arcade
- Apple New+
3. Follow the step by step instructions on the screen to join.

The feature you use will determine if you will be asked to set up an Apple Music family membership or an iCloud Storage subscription. If you share iTunes Store, App Store and Apple Books purchases with members of the group, you also have to pay for any item they buy while they are members of the group.

Creating an Apple ID for your child

1. Tap Settings ⚙ > [your name] > Family Sharing > Add Family member
2. Touch Create a Child Account and follow all the step by step instruction

The child's account is included in the family until the child is up to 13 years old.

Accepting an invitation to join a Family group
Press Accept or if you are close to the organizer when he/she is setting up the family group, insert your Apple ID and password on the Family Member's Apple ID screen on the organizer's device.

Vacate Family Sharing
Other members of the group can leave but the only the organizer can abort family sharing.

1. Tap Settings ⚙ > [your name] > Family sharing > [your name].
2. Touch Leave Family.

As the organizer, just press Stop Family Sharing to delete the group.

How to Share items you bought with family members

The organizer pays for items purchased from the iTunes Store, App Store or Apple Books. As soon as an item is purchased by a family member, the family organizers account is charged automatically. The purchases can be shared with the other family members in the group.

iTunes Store: How to access shared purchases

1. Launch the iTunes Store ⭐ > press More > tap Purchases.
2. Select a family member
3. Select a category (for instance, Movies) > Purchased item > press ☁ to download it.

App Store: How to access shared purchases

1. Launch App store 🅰
2. Press 👤 or your profile photo at the top right side of your screen.
3. Press Purchased > select a family member > touch ☁ next the purchased item to download it.

Apple Books: How to access shared purchases

1. Launch Books app 📖
2. Press 👤 or tap your profile photo at the top right side of your screen.
3. Select a family member > press category.

4. Touch All Books or Recent Purchases or Genre > press this icon ⛅ to download the purchased item.

How to share iCloud storage plan with members of your family

The Family Sharing feature allows you to share an iCloud storage plan of 200 GB or 2 TB with family members of the group.

1. Tap Settings ⚙ > [your name] > Family Sharing.
2. Press iCloud Storage > follow the prompts that appear on the screen.

You can buy or make use of your storage plan if you want more space.

Even when you are using Family Sharing, you can also hide your iTunes Store, App Store, and Apple Books from other family members.

1. Tap Settings ⚙ > [your name] > Family Sharing.
2. Touch Purchase Sharing > switch off Share My Purchases.

Using a shared Apple Music family membership

Follow these steps to sign up for Apple Music family membership. However, if your family already has an Apple Music family membership, you don't need to sign up.

1. Tap Settings ⚙ > [your name] > Family Sharing.
2. Press Apple Music > follow the prompts.

Every family member will get their library and personal recommendations. If you want to listen to music, log in with the Apple ID you used during the Family Sharing settings.

Using shared Apple News+ subscription

To learn about trending news, subscribe to Apple News+. It has more than 200 magazines and various publications. If you purchase an Apple News+ subscription, every member of the group will have access to the News and publication without paying any additional charge. You can subscribe through the News app. However, this feature is not available in all locations.

Using Shared Apple Arcade subscription

All the Family members can share subscription to Apple Arcade. This service is not available in all countries. With this subscription, you can access games that don't have ads. All the Arcade games can be accessed by the 6 members in the group from the App Store.

Using a shared subscription to Apple TV+ and Apple TV channels

The Family Sharing feature allows all the family members in the group to share subscriptions to Apple TV+ and Apple TV channels. However, this feature is not available in every location. Family members can watch the various channels with their iPhone. Just log in with your Apple ID and password to watch the various channels. One family member can subscribe to Apple TV+ Apple TV and every member of the family will have access.

Sharing pictures, calendar and so much more with family members

Family Sharing allows family members to share pictures, location, calendar, and lots more.

Sharing pictures or videos with family members on your iPhone

Upon setting up a Family Sharing feature, a shared album known as Family will be created instantly. Members of the group can share videos and pictures via this group.

1. Launch the Photos App > choose a picture or video

2. Touch ⬆️ > press Shared Albums.
3. Insert a comment > press Shared Album
4. Select an album where you want to add the picture or video.

Members of the Family Sharing can withdraw from the group while the organizer can delete or remove it.

Include an event to the family calendar

Upon setting up Family Sharing, a shared Family calendar will be created instantly on all members of the group's Calendar. You can insert events on the Calendar and allow other members of the group to see it.

1. Launch Calendar app 🗓️ > add events.
2. When you are adding events > tap Calendar > press Calendar and Family to include an event to the family calendar.

You can exit the group if you choose and the family organizer can remove the family calendar.

Sharing your location with family members

The Family Sharing feature allows other members of the group to view your location. The organizer's location is shared instantly with all the members of the group.

Other family members in the group can view your location in Find My 💿 Messages. However, you have to share your location for them to view it. Sharing your location can help you locate your iPhone if it gets lost.

The Location Services must be turned on in Settings > then tap Privacy to share your location.

1. Tap Settings > [your name] > Family Sharing > Location Sharing > switch on Share My Location.
2. Press Change My Location to This iPhone.

3. Touch the family member you want to share your location with, press Share My Location > hit this ⟨ button.

If you want to share your location with all the members in the group, you have to repeat the steps. Each family member will receive a notification informing them that you want to share your location. They can also choose to share theirs with you.

You can also share your location via the Messages app ⬤. Just touch the profile photo or name > tap ⓘ > press Send My Current Location or Share My Location.

If you don't want to share your location with a family member again tap Settings > [your name] > Share My Location > touch the family member > press Stop Sharing My Location.

If you want to view a family member's location, use the Find My app.

Sharing your Hotspot
It's possible to share your hotspot with other family members using Family Sharing. If any family member sets up a personal hotspot, members of the group can connect to the Hotspot with any password.

Activating Screen Time for family members on your device
With Family Sharing feature, you can set-up Screen Time for members of your family in the group. Apart from setting up Screen Time, you can set-up downtime, allowances for app use, and so on. Screen Time informs you and other family members how they are using their device. This information will help you structure how you are using your device.

The organizer of the group can send out an invite to other members. If you receive the invite, enter your Apple IDs and you are good to go.

Note: Setting up Screen time via Family Sharing means that every family member in the group will receive alerts about their weekly report. To view the alerts, just touch when they appear on your screen.

1. Tap Setting ⚙ > insert [your name] > Family Sharing > Screen Time
2. Touch the profile of a family member and press Turn on Screen Time.
3. Press Continue and follow the onscreen prompts.

Important: if you forget your family Screen Time passcode, use your device passcode via Touch ID or Face ID to reset it with your iPhone.

How to restart, update restore and reset your iPhone?
The regular iPhone user may not find the need to read this part. However, remember that settings keep changing.

How to turn on or off your iPhone
If you want to turn off the iPhone, do the following;

- Press and hold the side button and the volume button until sliders display on the screen

Or

- Tap Settings ⚙ > press General > Shut Down > drag the slider slowly.

If you want to turn it on, touch and hold the side button until the Apple logo displays on the screen.

Force restart

If you want to forcefully restart the iPhone, do any of the following;

- Press volume up button and release your hold as fast as possible
- Press the volume down button and release your hold as fast as possible
- Press and hold the side button. Release your hold when the Apple logo appears on the screen.

How to update iOS on your iPhone

Updating iOS on your iPhone doesn't affect your existing settings.

Note: Don't start the process of updating your iOS without setting up automatic back on your device manually.

How to set up an automatic update of your iPhone iOS

To turn on automatic updates, tap Settings > General > Software Update > tap Automatic Updates, switch on Automatic Updates.

Your device will install updates wirelessly. However, you will be alerted before the updates commence. To view the recent iOS updates that were installed, tap Settings > General > then touch Software Update.

How to set up manual updates on your iPhone

Tap Settings > touch the General icon > Software Update > Automatic Updates > switch off Automatic Updates.

You can install software updates by yourself at any time. Just tap Settings > General > Software Update. You will be notified of the recent updates that were made and if another update is available.

How to set up updates using your computer

1. Plug your iPhone to your computer via a USB cable.

Then carry out any of these actions;

- ***In the Finder sidebar on your Mac***: choose your iPhone device > click on General on the topmost part of the window.

Note: If you want to use Finder to update your device, you must get macOS Catalina.

- ***In the iTunes app on your Windows PC***: Click on the iPhone icon close to the top left corner of the iTunes window and tap Summary.
2. Tap Check for Update.
3. Click Update to start the installation.

How to back up your iPhone
You can either use iCloud or your computer to back up your iPhone.

Tip: Backing up your iPhone will help you store information your device and transfer the same to a new one if the need arises.

How to back up your iPhone with iCloud

1. Tap Settings ⚙ > enter [your name here] > iCloud > iCloud Back up.

2. Switch on the iCloud backup feature. Your data will be backed up by iCloud automatically daily when your device is connected to power and Wi-Fi.

3. If you want to back up your device manually, press Back Up Now.

If you want to view iCloud backups, tap Settings > insert [your name] > tap iCloud > Manage Storage > Backups.

On the other hand, if you will like to delete back up, press the Delete Backup button.

How to back up iPhone with your Mac

1. Plug your iPhone to your computer with a USB cable

2. Choose iPhone on the Finder sidebar

3. Click General at the top side of the Finder window

4. Choose Back up all of the data on your iPhone to this Mac.

5. If you want additional protection, you can encrypt your backup with a password. Tap Encrypt local backup

6. Click Back Up Now.

Note: Set up Wi-Fi syncing to connect your iPhone to your PC without a USB cable.

If you want to view the backup stored on your PC, select Edit > Preferences > Devices. Backups that are encrypted always have a lock sign on them.

How to return your iPhone settings to default

You don't need to erase your content, just return iPhone settings to default.

On the other hand, before you return your settings to default, you can save it. If your aim of returning to default setting is to solve a problem and it doesn't work, you can restore your previous settings from a backup.

1. Tap Settings > General > Reset
2. Select an option

Warning: Selecting the Erase All Content and Setting option means that all your content will be deleted.

- **Reset All Settings**: Clicking this option means returning all the setting on your iPhone to default. This includes network settings, location settings, privacy settings, Home screen layout, and Apple Pay cards are deleted. However, your media and data will remain intact.
- **Reset Network Settings**: All your network settings are removed. This will disconnect you from any Wi-Fi network or any other network you are connected to.
  If you want to remove VPN settings installed on your device, tap Settings > General > Profiles & Device Management > touch the configuration profile and tap Remove Profile.
  If you want to remove the network settings on MDM, tap Settings > General > Profiles & Device Management > touch Remove Management to delete the management.
- **Reset Keyboard Dictionary**: If you choose this option, it will erase all the words you have added in your dictionary settings.
- **Reset Home Screen Layout**: This option returns the apps on your device to their original layout on your Home screen.
- **Reset Location & Privacy**: Returns the location services to their default settings.

How to restore all the contents from your backup to iPhone

To restore content, settings and apps after you returned the iPhone settings to default, you need to back up these files with your PC or in iCloud.

How to restore iPhone from iCloud backup

1. Switch on the new or erased iPhone
2. Stick with the online prompts to select a language and region
3. Press Set Up Manually
4. Hit the Restore from iCloud Backup tab and follow the prompts on the screen.

You need to enter your Apple ID.

How to restore iPhone from a computer back up

1. Plug your erased or new iPhone to a computer with a USB. The computer should contain your backup.

Follow these steps;

- In the Finder Sidebar on your Mac: tap your iPhone and click Trust.
- In the iTunes app on a Windows PC: If more than one device is connected to your computer, choose the new or erased iPhone.

2. Click Restore from this backup > select the backup from the list > click Continue.

If your backup is encrypted, insert the password to unlock the files.

How to get rid of content and settings from your device

Some iPhone users don't know that deleting data on their device doesn't mean you can't access it again. It remains in the iPhone storage. If you want to completely remove all content, erase the iPhone memory.

For instance, if you want to sell or give your iPhone to another person, make sure you erase your iPhone.

1. Tap Settings ⊚ > General > Reset
2. Hit the Erase All Content and Settings icon.

When you restart the iPhone, you can either restore it from your backup or start afresh.

How to use various apps

What makes the iPhone 11 fun, is the numerous and advanced apps that are available. You can't be too eager to fire up iPhone 11 apps without carefully reading the instructions.

If you have never used an iPhone before, you will be blown away by the numerous apps it offers. You also have the privilege of buying more at the Apple Store. However, the aim of this chapter is to give you a guide of how to use the various inbuilt apps such as Face ID, Smart HDR, camera, Animoji and Memoji on the iPhone 11.

App basics

The part will help you with the fundamental features that you need. Unlike other iPhones, iPhone 11 doesn't have a Home Screen button. You will learn how to move around the various apps.

How to switch between Apps?

Use the App Switcher to switch to another app. If you switch, you will also pick up from where you stopped. Follow these steps below;

- Tap the App Switcher to see all your open apps.
- Swipe up from the bottom edge and stop in the middle of the screen.
- If you want to check out open apps, swipe to the right.

How to move and organize your app?

This feature helps you organize your app so that you easily locate it. Use the following method to move and rearrange your apps.

1. Touch and hold an app on the screen until it shakes.
2. Then drag it to any location of your choice.

You can also create a folder to group all your apps easily.

1. Touch and hold any app until it shakes.
2. Drag the app onto another application.
3. Then drag other apps to the folder.

If you want to name or rename, press the name field and insert the name of your choice.

To delete a folder, drag all the apps in the folder and the folder will be deleted immediately.

Lastly, to reset the Home screen to the previous setting, go to Settings > General > Reset. Then press Reset Home Screen Layout.

How to sign in with Apple on your iPhone

The Sign in with Apple feature allows to login to participating apps and websites using your Apple ID. With your Apple ID, you don't need to fill out lengthy forms or create a new password.

The Sign in with Apple feature helps to protect your privacy. The Apps and websites usually request your name and email address to create an account. Apple doesn't track you as you use the apps and websites.

How to create an account and log in

Whenever a participating app or website request that you create an account to log in as a first-time user, follow these steps;

1. Press the Sign in with Apple button.
2. Follow the onscreen prompts.

Most apps and websites may not ask for any private information. If that's the case, just authenticate with your Face Id or Touch ID to use the app.

Meanwhile, others may request details such as name and email address to create a personalized account. If the app request for such information, sign in with Apple will show your name and your email address from your Apple ID account. Review it to ensure that it is correct.

If you want to edit your name, press it and make the changes.

If you want to specify an email address, do the following;

3. Use your email address: Press Share My Email.

If you have more than one email address linked to your Apple ID, select the address of your choice.

Hide your email address: Press Hide My Email.

If you choose this option, apply will set up a special anonymized address that will forward email from your app to personal address. You can get emails from the app without disclosing your private email address.

When you have gone through the information you have provided, press Continue, to start using the app.

Sign in to start using your account
After creating an app or website using Sign in with Apple, you don't need to login to your iPhone again. However, if you are asked to sign in, follow these steps;

1. Press the Sign in with Apple icon.
2. Ensure that the Apple ID that pops up is correct > hit the Continue button to proceed.
3. Confirm with Face ID or Touch ID.

Altering the address used to send the email
If you have two or more address linked to your Apple ID, you can change the address that will receive the forwarded emails.

1. Tap Settings > insert [your name] > enter Phone numbers > Email > Forward to
2. Select another email and press Done.

How to change Sign in with Apple set up for an app or website
1. Tap Settings > [your name] > Password and Security.
2. Press Apps Using Your Apple ID.

When you select an app and then do any of the following;

- Turn off forwarding email: Switch off Forward To. As soon as this done, you will no longer receive emails from the app
- Stop using Sign in with Apple: Press Stop Using Apple ID. If you choose this option, then you may have to set up a new account whenever you attempt to sign in with the app again.

App Store

The typical iPhone user will have no need for this section. Notwithstanding, this book was written on the assumption, that you're using an iPhone for the first time. Just like the heading implies, you can purchase apps from the App Store.

However, you need an Apple ID to sign into the app store.

To find an app, tap Today, at the top right tap 👤 and enter your Apple ID.

You can enter the name of the app on the search tab.

If you want to buy an app, tap the price tag. This sign ☁ means that you bought this app before and so you can download it again without paying.

Tap ⚫ and then press Share App or Gift App.

How to download, view and set restrictions for app purchases?

Tap Today, then your profile picture and tap Purchased to view the app you bought.

If the Family Sharing is turned on, press My purchases or select a family member to see the apps they purchased.

To download an app, search for the app you want to download and tap ⬇.

To set up app restriction, Go to Settings > Screen Time > Content and Privacy Restrictions.

Books

If you love reading books, then you will lots of them to read. However, they are not free, you have to buy most of them.

How to find and purchase a book? - You can tap the Search tab to find a particular book.

Read a preview of the book or you can include it to your Want to Read collection.

Tap Buy to purchase a book.

How to read a book on the Books App? - Press Reading Now or Library button to read or see the book you are reading.

To bookmark a page, tap ⬜ . To view all your bookmarked pages, tap ☰.

How to listen to a book with Audiobook? - Press the audiobook cover to view the book you want to listen to. Use these buttons to control the audiobook.

☾ - Tap this icon to set the sleep timer.

≔ - Tap to move to another chapter.

To create a personalized library, tap Collections and tap New Collection.

You can name the collection and tap Done when you're through.

If you want to add a book to your collection, tap ⋯. Choose the collection and add the book.

To sort for a book, tap Library > Sort > Recent, title or author.

To remove a book tap Library > Edit > tap the item you want to remove, then tap 🗑 .

Camera

You can bet this is one of the interesting Apps on iPhone 11. The camera has several modes like Pano, Square, and Portrait, Live Photos, etc. You can either tap the Home Screen or swipe to the left hand side to open the camera from the Lock screen.

Take a Picture

To use the flash, tap ⚡ or you choose auto.

If you want to set a timer, frame your shot and stabilize your iPhone press ⌃ , touch 🕐 .

To do this on iPhone 11 toggle between 1x or 0.5x zoom out. To zoom in more than 2x, press and hold the zoom knob and drag the slider to the left side of the screen.

Meanwhile, on iPhone 11 Pro and iPhone 11 Pro Max, press the 2 button to zoom in and 5 to zoom out. If you want to zoom in more than 2x, press and hold the zoom knob and drag the slider to the left side.

To select a mode, swipe the screen to the left or right to choose a Photo, Video, Pano, Time-lapse, Slo-mo, and Portrait mode.

If you want to increase the field of view and take pictures inside the frame press 🔄. Touch the Shutter button or tap the volume up or down to take more pictures.

How to change your iPhone's camera focus and exposure

Your device camera is programmed to automatically set the focus and exposure. It also has a facial detection feature that balances the exposure across your face. To adjust the focus and exposure manually, follow these instructions;

1. Press the screen so that the automatic focus area and exposure setting will show.
2. Press where you want the focus area to go to.
3. Close to the focus area, drag ☀ icon up or down to alter the exposure.

You can also lock your manual focus and exposure set up for upcoming shots. To do this press and hold the focus area until it will pulse > press the screen to go back to automatic settings.

How to set up Night mode in low-light areas

If you are in a low-light area, you can use the Night mode feature to take bright and detailed shots. To set up night mode, do the following;

Usually, your camera is programmed to turn on Night mode in very low-light areas. Nonetheless, you can also turn it on manually.

Press ⏺ to turn on the Night mode feature in a low-light area.

Below the frame, you will see a slider that will display the auto recommended time. If you want to add more time press Max.

Press the Shutter icon > press and hold the camera firmly at a steady position until the timers count down to zero.

How to take a Panorama picture?
Select the Pano mode.

Press the Shutter button.

Pan gradually in the path of the arrow.

Tap the Shutter button to finish.

If you want to pan in the vertical direction, rotate the iPhone 11.

How to use a picture with a filter?

Select Photo, Square or Portrait mode tap ⌃ , then press ⚙.

Underneath the viewer, swipe the filters to the right or left.

How to take a photo in Portrait mode?
Select the Portrait mode.

Use the yellow portrait box to frame your subject.

Then press the Shutter button.

You can remove the Portrait mode effect on the iPhone 11.

How to adjust the Portrait Lighting?
This part of the iPhone 11 gives you the opportunity to edit your photo and add some studio touch.

Select the Portrait mode and frame your subject.

Choose from any of the following effects;

- **Natural light**: You can use this effect to sharpen the photo against a blurred background.
- **Studio light**: Used to brightly lit the photo and make it have a clean look.
- **Contour light**: Adds shadows with highlights and lowlights.
- **Stage light**: Adds a spotlight on the photo.
- **Stage light mono**: it has a similar stage light.
- **High-Key Light Mono**: To create a grayscale subject on a white background tap the High-key Light Mono button.

Note: You use Stage Light and Stage Light Mono when you front-facing TrueDepth camera.

How to adjust depth control on Portrait mode?
Select the Portrait mode and frame your subject.

Press 🅕 . You can find it at the top right hand of the screen.

Move the slider to the right to enhance the blur effect. If you want to reduce the blur effect, move the slider to the left.

Press the Shutter Button to take a picture.

How to take a Burst photo?
This feature will help you take a several photos in high-speed. That way, you can select the best and delete others. The rear and front cameras support this feature.

Select Photo or Square mode.

To take rapid shots, swipe the Shutter button to the left side of the screen.To stop, remove your finger.

Press the Burts thumbnail to choose the photos you like.

Press the circle in the bottom right corner of the photo you want to keep and press Done.

If you want to delete all the Burst, press the thumbnail and the delete sign 🗑 .

How to take a Live Photo?

This feature is spectacular. A Live Photo implies capturing the event that takes place before and after taking the photo, plus the audio.

Select the Photo mode.

Press ◎ to turn on Live photos.

Press the Shutter Button to take a photo.

To edit Live Photos, use the Photo app. To identify your Live Photos in your album, they are marked Live at the side.

Note: All images are in HDR (high dynamic range). This feature helps you get take high quality pictures. You can choose to turn on or off by going to Settings > Camera > Smart HDR. If you turn off HDR, the images will be normal.

Capturing content outside the camera frame on your device

If you are using iPhone 11, iPhone 11 Pro or iPhone 11 Pro Max, you can capture content outside the frame. This can be done when you take a shot or shoot a video to edit later in the Photos app.

Editing pictures and videos with content outside the frame

To edit pictures outside the frame, the Capture Outside the Frame has to be turned on. Contents that are captured outside the frame are seen when you are using crop and straighten to edit pictures in the Photo app.

If you want to capture content outside the frame, do the following

- Tap Setting ⚙ > Camera, switch on the Photos Capture Outside the Frame button.

- Recording Quick Take videos automatically activate the camera to capture content outside the frame. To switch it off, tap Settings > Camera, then turn off Videos Capture Outside the Frame.

Note: If you are using the content captured outside the frame to carry out your editing, the content will be deleted after thirty days.

Adjusting composition using the content outside the frame feature

The iPhone makes use of the content captured outside the frame to adjust a picture automatically or a QuickTake video to improve the composition. A blue Auto badge appearing at the top right side of the screen means that the automatic adjustment has been activated.

If you want to turn off automatic adjustments, tap Settings > Camera > turn off Auto Apply Adjustments.

Quickly capture video: This is a new feature that allows you to shoot a video quickly within the Photo mode. Just drag the shutter icon close to the camera switcher and it will switch to video recording automatically as soon as you let go.

The quick burst of photos: Just drag the shutter towards the camera roll to quickly grab some photos.

Switching between wide, ultra-wide and zoom: If you want to switch from one camera to another, press 1x showing on the screen. To zoom in or out, you can either swipe up or down on your screen.

Quick access to settings: While you are taking a picture, the need to get to Settings may arise. Swipe up above the shutter button and various options will appear on the screen including turning the flashlight on, enabling live photos, and so on.

Launching different camera modes in a jiffy: press and hold the camera app button for a while and the option to take a Portrait Selfie, Take Portrait, or Record a video will appear.

How to record a video?

Some people say that iPhone 11 is superb. You about to find out. To record a video do the following;

Select the video mode and tap 📷 to record a video.

You can take a picture while recording a video by pressing the white Shutter button.

To zoom in or out, tweak the screen. For a detailed zoom, press and hold 1x > drag the slider button to the left side of the screen. On iPhone 11, press 1x to zoom out, while on iPhone 11 Pro and iPhone 11 Pro Max, press 5 to zoom out.

You can either tap 📷 to stop or a Volume Button.

The default setting of the frame rate per second is 30 fps. Go to Settings > Camera >Record Video. If the frame rate is faster, it will increase the resolution of the video. The size of the video file will increase too.

Recording Videos in 4K using Any Rear sensor

Tap Settings > Camera > Record Video > tap 4K.

Recording 4K Video with your Selfie Camera

Using the same settings on the screen, you can change the resolution of the front-camera to 4K.

Note: By default, the iPhone is designed to record video in stereo. If you want to switch off stereo recording, tap Settings > Camera > toggle button to turn off Record Stereo Sound.

Recording a QuickTake video with your iPhone

Do you know that recording a QuickTake video in Photo mode is possible? You can also take still photos while the recording is going on. Just move the Record button into the lock position. You can do any of the following in QuickTake video;

1. In Photo mode, just press and hold the Shutter button to record a QuickTake video.
2. Slide the Shutter button to the right side and let go over the lock. This will enable hands-free recording
3. If you want to shoot a still photo, press the Shutter button while you are recording a QuickTake video.
4. To stop recording, press the Record button.

If you want to view QuickTake video in the Photo app, press the thumbnail.

How to record a video in slow-motion?

This camera mode has the tendency to make feel like you're shooting a movie. Here is how to use it;

Select the Slo-mo mode.

Press the Record button. You can also take a picture while the video is recording.

Press the video thumbnail and tap Edit to set a portion of the video to record in slow motion.

If you want to record in Slo-mo with the front-facing camera, press the .

Go to Settings > Camera > Record Slo-mo to change the settings.

How to take a time lapse video?

Select the Time-lapse mode.

Position the iPhone where you want to capture the event over the particular duration.

Press the record button to begin.

To zoom in tap ⬤1× and ⬤2× , then tap ⬤0.5× to zoom out.

To turn on Auto Low light FPS, go to Settings > camera > record video.

HDR - Go to Settings > Camera > turn on/off Smart HDR.

AE/AF Lock: Changing the exposure or focus of your photo is very easy. Just press anywhere on your screen and it will change immediately. If you want to lock the exposure or focus, long press anywhere on the screen until the square box locks in.

Change the exposure on the fly: When you discover your focus point in the Camera app, tap the small button and swipe up or down to alter the exposure settings. Press up for a brighter exposure and darker for a darker one.

How to view, share, and print photos?
All photos and videos are saved in your Photo app. If the iCloud Photos is turned on, every picture is uploaded and accessible from any device that is connected to the iCloud Photos.

To view Photos

Press the thumbnail image at the bottom of the left side.

You swipe to the right or left to view the images that you took.

Press the screen to display or hide the controls.

To share and print photos

Tap ⬆️.

Choose an option either Mail, Messages or Print.

Photos
To view photos and videos, use the Photo app.

You can go through your photo albums, memories, using Photos, Albums and the Search tabs.

Photos: Check out the pictures and videos on your device. They are organized according to the days, months and year they were taken.

For You: This is a personalized feed that displays all your memories, shared albums, and lots more.

Albums: Check out all the albums you created or shared. Conveniently, they are organized into various categories.

Search: You can search for your photos by date, place, or location. You can also browse photos you grouped in various categories.

You can carry out the following functions when you are viewing your photos in full screen;

- **Zoom in or out**: Tap the screen twice swiftly or pinch out to zoom in if it is zoomed in. you can also tap the screen twice swiftly to zoom out.

- **Share**: Press ⬆️ > select how you would like to share the photo

- **Add to favourites**: Press ♡ to include the photo to your Favorite album.

Choose any video or video and swipe up to view the following;

- Effects that are available and can be added to a Live Photo
- People that known in your photo

- The location the photo was shot
- A link to see other photos that were shot nearby

Merging People in the Photo app

Your device can browse through photos and identify people and places. If the Photo app has picked out a particular individual but says that they are not the same person, you can merge the album yourself.

Tap Photos app > Albums > choose People & Places > then press Select at the top right side of the screen > choose the photos of the people you want to merge > press the Merge button.

How to delete people in Photos app

Just tap Photos app > Album > choose People & places. If you want to delete, press Select and touch the people you want to remove and then tap Remove button at the bottom left of your screen.

Sharing Memories movie

Apple Photos app usually sets up a mini slideshow for you to share (that's if you want to). To share a memory, go to Memory in the For you tab > press Play > touch the share button.

Altering the style of a Memories movie

You can choose the default movie style or use other styles. Tap the Memory you want to edit > press Play button on the photo > then press the video while it's playing. Various slideshow options such as Dreamy, Gentle and so on will appear. You can also select Short, Medium or Long.

Editing photos

Locate the photo you want to edit and press the Edit icon. It's on the top corner of the screen. To improve the outlook of the photo automatically you can either tap the volume button or tap the wand.

Straighten out your photos

To carry out this function, Choose the cropping tool > Edit > move the dial that will show on your screen.

Searching Photo albums

Open the Photo app and tap the magnifying glass. You can limit your search to One year ago, Favorites or Nearby. You can combine a search for places, names or months.

Tell Siri to get a Photo for you

Siri now can search for photos. You can limit your search to a specific date to get faster results.

Upload Photo Bursts

Tap Settings > enter your name at the topmost part of the screen > launch iCloud > Photos > Upload Burst Photos. This step backs up all your photos in burst instead of the favourite only.

Favourite photos

If they are photos you would like to show to friends and family, you can mark them or show them later. Look for your favourite photo on your device and tap the Heart button. If you want to find your favourite photos faster, on the Photo app > tap the Albums icons > then tap your Favorite Album.

Find out where you took your photo

On Albums > press People & Places > select Places album. All the places and locations where you took your photo will show. When you zoom in, you will get to see more specific locations > tap Grid to see locations in that view.

Turning on iCloud Photo Library

When this feature is turned on, it means that all your photos will be stored on iCloud automatically. Turn on the iCloud Photo Library to upload photos on iCloud.

FaceTime

The FaceTime app, allows you to make video and audio calls to your loved ones. It doesn't matter if they make use of an iOS or Mac device. The front camera of the iPhone 11 allows you to talk to the other person face to face. You can use the rear camera to show your environment to the other person.

The FaceTime features may not be available to some users residing in certain regions.

How to set up FaceTime?

Go to Settings > FaceTime and put it on.

To snap Live Photos while you making FaceTime calls, switch on the FaceTime Live Photos.

Insert your phone number, Apple ID, email address to access FaceTime.

Since the iPhone 11 has a Dual SIM, you change the phone you are using on FaceTime. Go to Settings > Messages > iMessage and FaceTime Line to select the network. You are not allowed to use more than one network.

How to make calls with FaceTime?

If you have your iPhone 11 connected to a Wi-Fi, a cellular data connection or an Apple ID, you can make and receive FaceTime calls. To use FaceTime via your cellular connection, go to Settings > Cellular > switch on FaceTime calls.

Press ＋ on FaceTime.

Insert the name or phone number you wish to call and press 􀍉 to make a video call. If you want to make an audio call, press 􀌾.

To make a group call on FaceTime, tap ＋ to add more persons by inserting their name, phone number or Apple ID. Assuming no one picks your call, you can press Leave a Message to drop a message or cancel the call.

You can set up a FaceTime call from a message conversation. Press ⓘ , touch the FaceTime tab.

You can either choose to accept a FaceTime call, decline, send a message or tap Remind Me.

How to manage FaceTime calls?

There are other functions that you can carry out while using FaceTime. You use other apps while you're making a FaceTime call or even blocked some calls. You can also take a FaceTime Live Photo while you are on a call with a friend.

To take a FaceTime Live Photo, touch ◯. However, you must ensure that the FaceTime Live Photo is turned on. To do this, go to Settings > FaceTime.

If you don't want a particular caller to call you, simply block their FaceTime calls.

Go to Settings > FaceTime > Blocked

Press Add New to add a particular contact to your blocked calls.

Press the contact you want to block.

To unblock a contact, tap unblock.

Files

This app allows you to open and view documents, images, etc., saved on iCloud drive. You can also view documents, images, etc., that are saved in storage providers like Box and Dropbox.

If you want to view a file or folder, just tap it to open it. Changing how files are sorted will help you know where to find your files. Press Sorted by to choose whether it will be sorted by name, date, size, etc.

To find a file or folder, do the following;

- Touch search and insert the name of the file
- Start the search
- Open the file.

To add a file to a cloud storage device, download an iCloud app from the Apple Store and follow the instructions.

- To switch the iCloud on, Go to Settings > iCloud > then put it on.
- Invite others to use the file on iCloud.

You can invite a friend to view a file on iCloud by sending them the link. You can also allow a friend who has the link to the file to edit it. All you have to do is;

- Tap the file
- Press Share and touch
- Select the method for sharing the link
  If you want to restrict a person from editing the document, tap View only.

Find My Friends

This app is a good way to find your friends and family who use iPad, iPad, iPhone, Apple Watch Series 3. You can share your location with them and it will appear on their map. You can also use this app to get notifications when your friends leave or arrive a location.

How to set location sharing?
Tap Settings > [your name] > then switch on Share My Location.

Choose the device you want to share your location with your friends.

Share Location with friends
Launch the Find My Friends app and do this;

Insert the name of the loved one you want to share your location with.

Choose the friend who appears in AirDrop and choose how long you want share the location.

Your friends or loved one will get a notification informing them that you want to share your location with them.

How to set notifications when your arrive at a location?
Choose a friend and press Notify Me.

You can choose if you want to receive notifications when your friend or loved one leaves or arrives a location.

Do you know that you can ask Siri to find out the friend that shared location with you.

Find My iPhone location

This feature or app helps you a locate your iPhone 11 if it gets stolen. The Find My iPhone app has a feature known as Activation Lock. This feature ensures that nobody can make use of your iPhone 11, except you or without your permission. However, before this app can work effectively, the Find My Device app must be turned on. The iPhone must have internet access.

How to activate Find My iPhone?
Tap Settings >[your name] > iCloud > Find My iPhone

Switch on Find My iPhone.

Turn on the Send Last Location. This will enable the iPhone 11 to send it last before the battery runs out.

How to find your iPhone 11?
Open Find My iPhone on another iOS device or via a PC. On your computer, go to Find My iPhone app on iCloud.

Log in your Apple ID. Choose the device you want to find.

Press Action then touch any of the following options;

- Play sound
- Lost mode
- Erase your missing device

Each of these functions will either make the missing iPhone to play a sound even if it's in silent mode, lock your iPhone with a passcode or erase the entire iPhone memory and set it back to default settings. Either of these modes will make the iPhone useless for the thief.

iTunes
The iTunes Store app helps you add music, movies, TV Shows to your iPhone 11. If you reside in some regions, renting movies is permitted.

To have access to these files, you must have an internet connection and an Apple ID. Using iTunes is not permitted in some regions.

How to find music, movies, and so on?
- Press either, Music, Movies, or TV shows
- Insert the name of what you are looking for in the search tab
- Touch the result to get more information.

How to share music, movies, TV shows, etc.?
- Press ⬆ to pick a sharing option
- To add to Wish list, press ⬆ and touch Add to Wish List.

If you like a song playing you, just ask Siri, what song is playing. Siri will provide the name of the song, artist, and other relevant information.

How to buy and download content?
Press price, and touch buy.

If this sign ☁ appears instead of price, it means you have bought the item before.

You can check out the progress of the download by taping more.

How to rent movies?
Each movie lasts for 30 days to watch. You can play it so many times within 48 hours after watching the movie. As soon as the rental period expires, the movie will be deleted.

- Press the movie rental price
- Press Rent.

You can either stream the movie or download it.

You can continue to stream or downloading on another device, log in your iTunes ID and Apple ID.

How to redeem or give an iTunes gift?
- Press Music
- Scroll down a little
- Press Redeem or Send Gift.

Managing your iTunes Store
You can manage how purchases are made from your iTunes. This is very important with regards to purchases that are made within a restricted age in Family Sharing. Family sharing allows you to review and approve items bought by other family members.

- Press More and touch Purchased.

If the Family Sharing is activated, pick a family member to view the items they have bought. (this is possible only when the family member decides to share their purchases with you).

- Press Music, Movies, or TV shows
- Look for the item you want to download. Press ☁.

To view your entire purchase, tap Purchase history.

Changing iTunes Store Settings
- Tap Settings > [your name] >iTunes and App Store to change your settings.

Apple Music

This is one of the interesting features that iPhones are known for. There is more to this feature than playing and purchasing music.

Hide Apple Music
You can hide Apple Music. See how it is done. Tap Settings > Music > then turn off Show Apple Music. If you go to the Apple Music app, only your music will show. Music that is available for purchase will not appear. This feature has been around since iOS 12.

Learn the best way to reach your entire music library
To view on the songs, albums, playlist, etc. press the Library button. You can find it on the app's menu bar close to the bottom. You will also get to see songs that you purchased from iTunes, songs ripped from CD's and so on.

Editing your Library categories
If you want to clear your library and specify that categories of the library you would like to see at a glance, just press Edit > then turn on or off.

Finding your downloaded music
Press the Library button on the app's menu bar on the bottom > then touch Download Music.

Creating a new playlist
Are you planning on going on a road trip? Then it's time to create a playlist. Press the Library button > touch Playlists > tap New Playlist > enter your preferred playlist name > tap on or off to make the playlist public.

Searching for Apple's curated playlists
To find music that was selected by Apple Music team go to the For You tab. Some of the suggestions include daily playlists, new releases, and artist spotlights. The music that will appear is targeted at your music preferences.

Searching for Apple Music

Simply press the Search button to insert name of the artist, album titles and so on. To make the search result appear quickly, you can also use the lyrics to search for the music.

Searching for top music charts

Tap the Browse button on the menu bar > press Top Charts to view the updates of the most popular songs on Apple Music.

Finding top music charts by genre

Usually, the Top Charts section in the Browse tab displays all the genres of music. You select any genre of your choice by scrolling down until More to Explore appears.

How to find videos

Apple Music is not about music alone. You can find music videos here too. Tap the Browse tab on the menu bar and scroll down to the Music Videos tab.

Finding the Beats 1 radio station

Apple Music has a radio station known as Beats 1. This radio station streams live 24/7. To access it, press the Radio button > then touch the Beat 1 knob.

How to search for radio stations

They are other radio stations that are offered by Apple Music other than Beat 1. Go to the Radio tab menu close to the bottom. However, other radio stations are categorized into various genres. Just pick the genre that will suit you.

Sharing an album

Sharing an album via Facebook, Twitter, or any other platform is possible with your device. Press the album > tap the button with the (...) > press Share album > then choose how you want to share the album.

Adding an album to a Play Next queue

With you Apple Music, you can queue up albums you will like to listen with this app. All you need to do is add is to your Play Next list. Choose an album > tap the button with the (...) > touch Play Next.

Adding an album to your playlist

To add an album to a playlist, press the album >choose the button with the (...) > press Add to a Playlist > pick the playlist to want to add the album too.

Download an album to your Library to listen offline

Touch the album > choose the (...) button > press Add to a Library > you will be taken back to the album screen > touch the button that resembles a cloud.

How to like or dislike an album

If you want Apple Music to provide more suggestions of music to you, you can either love or dislike an album. Press an album > tap the (...) button > touch Love or Dislike button depending on what you prefer.

Creating a station from a song

Choose any song > tap the music control menu on the bottom to expand it to full screen > tap the (...) button > touch Create Station > a radio station will be set up based on that song choice.

Sharing a Song

You can share a song through Facebook, Twitter or any other social media platform. Touch the Song > tap the bottom of the music controls menu to expand into full screen > tap the (...) button > touch Share Album > choose how you want to share the song.

Adding songs to Play Next queue

You can use this option to queue up songs you will love to listen to. All you have to do is add it to your Play Next list. Touch the song > tap the bottom of the music control menu to expand to full screen > tap the (...) button > press Play Next button.

Adding songs to your playlist

Choose any song of your choice by tapping on it > tap the bottom of the music control menu to expand to full-screen card >tap the (...) button > Press Add to a Playlist choose a playlist.

Downloading songs to Library for offline listening

Press on your song preference > Tap + to include it to your library > then touch the cloud download tab.

How to find the lyrics of a song

If you can't hear the lyrics of a song, you can take a look at the lyrics in Apple Music. Touch the song > tap the bottom of the music control menu to expand to full-screen card > tap the icon that looks like a speech bubble. It also has a quotation mark inside it.

Share an artist

If you like the song or album of a particular artist, you can also share it with friends and family members through Facebook, Twitter or any other platform. Touch on the artist page (you can search for the artist by inserting his/her name on the search tab) > press the (...) button near the artist name > tap Share Artist > and select which medium you will like to share the artist songs with.

Safari

When you are using the Safari browser on your device, below are a few functions that you may not know were available;

How to prevent websites from tracking you: Tap Settings > Safari > tap the Prevent cross-site tracking to turn it on.

How to access saved passwords: With Safari, you can save passwords across various devices. This is possible because of iCloud. To do this tap Settings > Passwords & Accounts > Website & App Passwords > sign in with your Face ID scanner. All the passwords that were stored will appear.

How to search a Page in Safari: If you are looking for a particular text on a Safari page, tap the Share icon and a Find on Page option will appear.

How to disable frequently visited sites in Safari: If you observe closely, you will realize that Safari usually displays icons of your frequently visited websites whenever you open a new page. You can delete them one after the other if you tap and hold on them. If you want to switch off this feature, tap Settings > Safari > tap Frequently Visited Sites to turn it off.

DuckDuckGo: To set up DuckDuckGo as your default search engine instead of Google or Yahoo, tap Settings > Safari > Search Engine > then choose private friendly search engine as the default.

Activate/deactivate the auto-suggesting website feature: Safari can also recommend search result as you type the text too. This feature is usually on default, but you can remove it if you want. Tap Settings > Safari > Search Engine Suggestions > toggle to turn it off.

Auto suggesting apps: As part of Safari's default settings, it usually suggests app names when you enter a text into the Safari search URL box. To turn it off, tap Settings > Safari > Safari Suggestions, then toggle it to switch off.

How to make your website load fast and useless data: Safari usually preloads search results. This can cause an increase in data usage. To switch it off, tap Settings > Safari > Preload Top Hit > toggle to turn it off.

How to scan your credit card: You don't need to waste time typing all in all your details. Use your camera to scan the details of your credit card. Tap Auto-Fill to use the Keychain feature or tap Auto-Fill > press Use Camera to scan your credit card details.

Reminders

The Reminder app helps you to create a notification that will remind you of your various appointments and activities. You can create a shopping list subtask, add attachments and so on.

How to create a reminder

You can ask Siri. For instance, you can say Add rice to my shopping list or you can follow these steps;

1. Press New Reminder the inserted text.
2. You can use the quick toolbar above the keyboard to carry out any of the following;

- *Set a date or time*: Press , tap the date for reminder or press Custom to set up a date and time for the reminder.

- *Insert location*: Press > select the location where you want the notification. For instance, you can choose when you leave the office or get back home.

- *Set a Flag*: Press to mark an important reminder.

- *Attach a picture or a document*: Press to shoot a new picture or select a photo from your library or scan a document.

If you want to include more details to the reminder, press and do any of the following;

- **Add notes**: Add more details about the reminder in the Notes field.
- **Add a website link**: You can insert a website address in the URL field. The reminders will show the link as thumbnails so you can click on it to visit the site.
- **Receive a reminder when chatting with someone in Messages**: Switch on the Remind me when messaging > then select anybody from your contact list > the reminder will show up whenever you chat with the person via Messages.
- **Set a Priority**: Press Priority then select any option > tap Done.

How to mark a reminder as complete

Touch the empty circle close to the reminder. This will automatically hide all the completed reminders that have been

marked. If you want to view completed reminders, press ••• > touch the Show Completed button.

Rearrange or delete a reminder

- **Reorder reminders in a list**: Press and hold the reminder you want to move to a new location. Drag it to your preferred location.
- **Make a subtask**: Swipe right on the reminder > press Indent or drag a reminder over another one.
  Whenever the parent task is deleted, the subtask will also be deleted. If you complete a parent task, the subtask will also be completed.
- **Move a reminder to a different list**: Press reminder > touch the (i) icon > press List > select a list.
- **Delete a reminder**: Swipe to the left side on the reminder > press Delete.

If you want to recover a reminder that was deleted, shake your device to undo or swipe to the left side of the screen with your 3 fingers.

How to change the iPhone Reminder settings

To alter the iPhone reminder settings, do the following;

1. Tap Settings ⚙ > Reminders
2. Select any of the options below;

- *Default List:* select the new reminders you created outside a specific list. Reminders you created using Siri fall into this category.
- *Today Notification:* Schedule the time you want a notification in Today View for all-day reminders that are assigned dates without time to display.
- *Show Reminders as Overdue:* The set date for all-day reminders that are overdue turns red.

How to use smart lists

Smart lists help you to keep track of upcoming reminders. It also helps you organize the reminders too. Underneath the search field press any of the following;

- *Today:* View reminders that are set up for today and overdue
- *Scheduled*: View reminders that are scheduled by date or time
- *Flagged:* View reminders that are flagged as crucial
- *All:* View all the reminders notwithstanding the list.

There are *other brilliant apps such as* Calculator, Calendar, Clock, Compass, Contacts, Health, Maps, Messages, TV, etc.

Do you need help?

Below are simple tips that you should try out first before you visit an authorized Apple service shop.

Black or a frozen screen

If your screen has become frozen or turned black, you may need to force a restart. Don't be scared, a forced restart will not delete the contents on your device. To force a restart, press and quickly release Volume Up button. Then press and quickly release the Volume Down button. Also, press and hold the Side button until the Apple logo appears.

Note: After a forced restart and the device is not turning on, do the following;

- Plug your iPhone to a power source and allow it to charge for about an hour or more.
- Ensure that the charging screen appears
- If the charging screen doesn't appear within an hour, check the jack or USB cable. Ensure that it is plugged in properly and not damaged.
- If it doesn't turn on, try another power adapter.

The device is on but gets stuck during start-up

If an apple logo or red or blue screen appears when starting your device, do any of the following;

- Plug in your iPhone to a PC with a USB cable. If you are using a Mac with macOS Catalina 10.15, launch Finder. If using a Mac with macOS Mojave 10.14 or a PC, launch iTunes
- Find your device on your PC
- While the iPhone is plugged into your computer, press and quickly release the Volume Up button. Long press and release the Volume Down button. Then long press and hold the Side button until the recovery mode screen appears

- If the option to restore or update appears, select Update. Your PC will reinstall iOS or iPadOS without deleting your contents
- Your computer will download the software for your iPhone. If the process takes more than 15 minutes, your iPhone will exit the recovery mode and you have repeat step 2 and 3.

Difficulty connecting to a Wi-Fi network

- Ensure that your router is properly connected and within range
- Ensure that the Wi-Fi is turned on and your network is visible
- Tap Settings > Wi-Fi and toggle the button on. Tap the name of your Wi-Fi. When a blue checkmark appears close to the Wi-Fi network, it means that you are connected.
- Insert the Wi-Fi password if requested
- If an Unable to join the network message or Incorrect Password message appears, restart the device and insert the password again
- Check if your Wi-Fi has any issues
- If iOS discovers an issue with your Wi-Fi network, a Wi-Fi recommendation will appear underneath the name of the Wi-Fi network that you are connected to. For instance, an alert like No Internet Connection may appear. For more details, press the Wi-Fi network
- Check out your cable's connection
- If you are still experiencing difficulties in connecting to your Wi-Fi network, check that your router is connected to your modem
- Restart your iPhone, router and the DSL modem.

If when the device is turned on and the issue persists, do any of the following;

- Reset your Network Settings. Touch Settings > General > Reset Network settings. The password of the Wi-Fi network will also reset including VPN and APN settings, and cellular settings you used earlier

- If your device is connected to the Wi-Fi is network but you are finding it difficult to use the internet, try using your Wi-Fi network with another device. If it still doesn't work, contact your cable company or internet provider
- Connect to a different Wi-Fi network in another location to see if the problem persists. If your iPhone still doesn't connect, then contact Apple
- You can also update your Wi-Fi router with the current firmware to ensure that it supports your device.

Difficulty in transferring content from an Android device to your iPhone

Are you having any challenge with moving content from an Android device? Do any of the following;

- Don't abort the transfers until it is completed. Any interference such as phone calls will affect the transfer. You can switch to flight mode to avoid any interference
- Turn off apps or settings that you think may affect your Android devices such as Sprint Connections Optimizer or the Smart Network Switch
- Restart the iPhone and Android device
- Switch off your mobile data connection on your Android device. Try the transfer again.

Note: If you notice that your iOS device is out of storage space, then you need to erase the contents on the device and start all over. Ensure that the contents on the Android device don't exceed the available space on your iPhone.

Recover your forgotten passwords, passcode and alerts

If you receive a notification to change your passcode or you are finding it difficult to adjust the passcode settings it may be as a result of view issues. Sometimes configuration profiles and email accounts from Microsoft Exchange has policies that cause issues such as;

- Difficulty in turning off your passcode
- An alert about a Passcode Requirement popping up. For instance, a prompt may appear requesting that you change your passcode within 60 minutes.

To avoid some of these issues, ensure that your iOS or iPadOs versions are up to date.

Forgotten Passcode
Inserting the wrong passcode so many times will cause your device to temporarily disable itself.

If you forget your passcode, then you are left with no option than to erase your device. All your settings and contents will be erased. You can only retrieve them if you had a backup. To remove your passcode, you need a computer to complete these steps or you can visit an Apple authorized Service Provider.

1. Long press and hold the Side button and either the up or down volume buttons until the power slider shows on the screen. Drag the slider to switch your iPhone. Then connect your iPhone to your computer while you are holding the Side button. Hold on to the Side button until the recovery mode appears on the screen.
2. Look for your device on the computer. If the option to Restore or Update appears, select Restore. Finder or iTunes will automatically download software for your device. If this process takes more than 15 minutes, your device will exit recovery mode automatically. Repeat the steps!
3. Allow the process to be completed before you start using your iPhone.

Note: If you forget the restriction passcode you set up on your previous iOS version you may need to erase your device. You have to do the same thing if you forget your Screen Time passcode.

Made in the USA
Las Vegas, NV
22 June 2021

25254045R00066